W9-AOF-197

My Path to Math

1 2 3 4 5 6 7 8 9

TIME

Penny Dowdy

Crabtree Publishing Company

www.crabtreebooks.com

Author: Penny Dowdy
Coordinating editor: Chester Fisher
Series editor: Susan Labella
Editors: Reagan Miller, Molly Aloian
Proofreader: Crystal Sikkens
Project coordinator: Robert Walker
Production coordinator: Margaret Amy Salter
Prepress technician: Margaret Amy Salter
Logo design: Samantha Crabtree
Cover design: Ranjan Singh (Q2AMEDIA)
Design: Neha Gupta (Q2AMEDIA)
Project manager: Kavita Lad (Q2AMEDIA)
Art direction: Dibakar Acharjee (Q2AMEDIA)
Photo research: Sejal Sehgal

Photographs:
Dreamstime: Dipa: p. 17
Fotolia: Sonya Etchison: p. 12 (right)
Ingram Photo Objects: p. 16
Istockphoto: Jacek Chabraszewski: p. 8; Grafissimo: p. 20;
    Bonnie Jacobs: p. 12 (left); Paul Kline: p. 1 (bottom),
    9 (bottom); Plus: p. 13; James Steidl: p. 6 (right)
Q2a Media: p. 15, 19, 21 (top and middle)
Shutterstock: Sonya Etchison: p. 5; Gelpi: p. 18 (top),
    21 (bottom); Igor Grochev: p. 6 (left); Anastasios
    Kandris: p. 10, 11; Pavel Losevsky: p. 1 (top), 9 (top);
    Donald P. Oehman: p. 4; OlgaLis: p. 7; Mark Szumlas:
    p. 14, 18 (bottom); Yakov Stavchansky: cover

Library and Archives Canada Cataloguing in Publication

Dowdy, Penny
    Time / Penny Dowdy.

(My path to math)
Includes index.
ISBN 978-0-7787-4344-6 (bound).--ISBN 978-0-7787-4362-0 (pbk.)

    1. Time--Juvenile literature. I. Title. II. Series: Dowdy, Penny.
My path to math.

QB209.5.D69 2008   j529   C2008-903485-6

Library of Congress Cataloging-in-Publication Data

Dowdy, Penny.
    Time / Penny Dowdy.
        p. cm. -- (My path to math)
    Includes index.
    ISBN-13: 978-0-7787-4362-0 (pbk. : alk. paper)
    ISBN-10: 0-7787-4362-4 (pbk. : alk. paper)
    ISBN-13: 978-0-7787-4344-6 (reinforced library binding : alk. paper)
    ISBN-10: 0-7787-4344-6 (reinforced library binding : alk. paper)
    1. Time--Juvenile literature. I. Title. II. Series.

    QB209.5.D69 2009
    529--dc22
                                                    2008023535

Crabtree Publishing Company

www.crabtreebooks.com   1-800-387-7650

Copyright © **2009 CRABTREE PUBLISHING COMPANY**. All rights reserved. No part of this publication may be reproduced, stored in a retrieval system
or be transmitted in any form or by any means, electronic, mechanical, photocopying, recording, or otherwise, without the prior written permission of Crabtree
Publishing Company.

Published in Canada
Crabtree Publishing
616 Welland Ave.
St. Catharines, Ontario
L2M 5V6

Published in the United States
Crabtree Publishing
PMB16A
350 Fifth Ave., Suite 3308
New York, NY 10118

Published in the United Kingdom
Crabtree Publishing
White Cross Mills
High Town, Lancaster
LA1 4XS

Published in Australia
Crabtree Publishing
386 Mt. Alexander Rd.
Ascot Vale (Melbourne)
VIC 3032

Contents

What is Time?

Time is a way we can measure things. Time measures how long something takes to happen. Time can measure how long it takes you to do things. Some things take a short amount of time. Other things take a long amount of time.

Brushing your teeth takes a short amount of time.

How much time do you spend brushing your teeth? How much time do you spend on the school bus? Which takes a longer amount of time?

Clocks

There are different tools to measure time. A
clock is used to measure time. It breaks a day
into smaller parts. A **watch** is a kind of clock.
Many people wear watches on their wrists.
Some clocks are on walls.

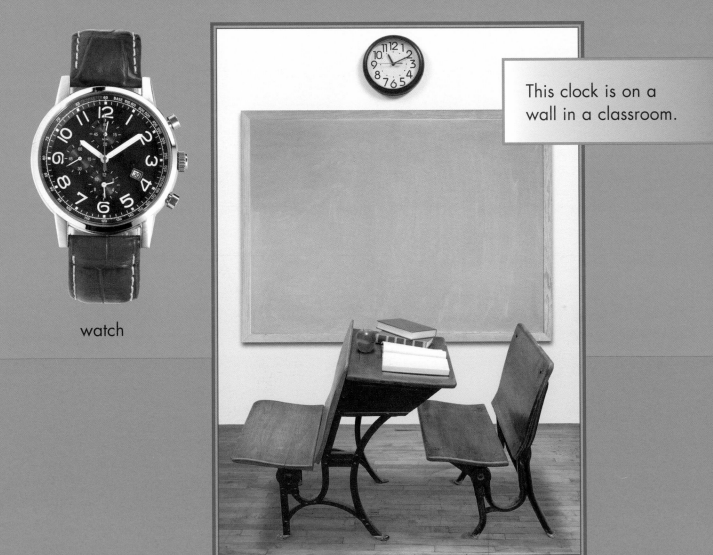

watch

This clock is on a
wall in a classroom.

Some clocks are huge! This big clock is on a building.

Parts of a Clock

The front of a clock is called the **face**. The face shows the numbers 1 to 12.

A clock has two **hands**. The hands point to the time. The short hand is called the **hour hand**. It points to the **hour** of the day. The long hand is called the **minute hand**. It points to the **minutes**. Some clocks have a long, thin hand called the **second hand**. It counts the seconds.

Activity Box

Point to each part of the clock. Name each part.

Second hand

Hour hand

Minute hand

face

A clock has hands like you!

Telling the Time

People tell time by counting hours and minutes. There are 60 minutes in an hour. The hour hand moves one number each hour. The hour hand on this clock is pointing to the number 2. We know it is 2 o'clock.

We start counting the hours at the top of the clock. The number 12 is at the top.

There are 60 seconds in a minute. The minute hand moves one mark each minute. There are five marks between each number. We can **skip count** by 5s to find out the minutes.

The minute hand on this clock points to the number 6. If we skip count to the number 6, we know it is 30 minutes.

To tell the time, we look at both the hour and minutes. On this clock, the hour hand is pointing to the number 2. The minute hand is pointing to the number 6. The time is 2:30.

Parts of a Day

There are 24 hours in a day. A day is split into different parts. These parts are called **morning**, **afternoon**, and **night**. We wake up in the morning. The morning is the start of the day. The afternoon follows the morning. When the sun goes down, it is night.

School starts in the morning.

People often eat lunch in the afternoon.

We get ready for bed at night.
Reading stories is a good way
to get ready for bed.

Calendars

A **calendar** is another tool to measure time. A calendar is a chart that shows days, weeks, and **months**.

There are 24 hours in one day. There are seven days in each week. The days of the week are:

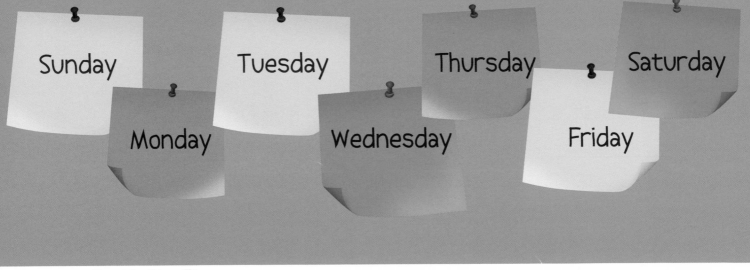

Sunday

Monday

Tuesday

Wednesday

Thursday

Friday

Saturday

Activity Box

Which days of the week do you go to school? Which days of the week do you stay home from school?

JUNE

SUNDAY	MONDAY	TUESDAY	WEDNESDAY	THURSDAY	FRIDAY	SATURDAY
1	2	3	4	5	6	7
8	9	10	11	12	13	14
15	16	17	18	19	20	21
22	23	24	25	26	27	28
29	30	1	2	3	4	5

This calendar shows the month of June.

15

Months

A calendar shows 12 months. A month is a part of a **year**. There are 12 months in one year. Look at the calendar on the next page. Read the name of each month.

The first day of a month begins with the number 1. Some months have 30 days. Other months have 31 days. One month has only 28 days.

Activity Box

Use the calendar on the next page. Point to the month of your birthday. Which day of the week is your birthday?

2009

Look at the calendar on this page. Can you find the month that has only 28 days?

January

Sun	Mon	Tue	Wed	Thu	Fri	Sat
				1	2	3
4	5	6	7	8	9	10
11	12	13	14	15	16	17
18	19	20	21	22	23	24
25	26	27	28	29	30	31

February

Sun	Mon	Tue	Wed	Thu	Fri	Sat
1	2	3	4	5	6	7
8	9	10	11	12	13	14
15	16	17	18	19	20	21
22	23	24	25	26	27	28

March

Sun	Mon	Tue	Wed	Thu	Fri	Sat
1	2	3	4	5	6	7
8	9	10	11	12	13	14
15	16	17	18	19	20	21
22	23	24	25	26	27	28
29	30	31				

April

Sun	Mon	Tue	Wed	Thu	Fri	Sat
			1	2	3	4
5	6	7	8	9	10	11
12	13	14	15	16	17	18
19	20	21	22	23	24	25
26	27	28	29	30		

May

Sun	Mon	Tue	Wed	Thu	Fri	Sat
					1	2
3	4	5	6	7	8	9
10	11	12	13	14	15	16
17	18	19	20	21	22	23
24	25	26	27	28	29	30
31						

June

Sun	Mon	Tue	Wed	Thu	Fri	Sat
	1	2	3	4	5	6
7	8	9	10	11	12	13
14	15	16	17	18	19	20
21	22	23	24	25	26	27
28	29	30				

July

Sun	Mon	Tue	Wed	Thu	Fri	Sat
			1	2	3	4
5	6	7	8	9	10	11
12	13	14	15	16	17	18
19	20	21	22	23	24	25
26	27	28	29	30	31	

August

Sun	Mon	Tue	Wed	Thu	Fri	Sat
						1
2	3	4	5	6	7	8
9	10	11	12	13	14	15
16	17	18	19	20	21	22
23	24	25	26	27	28	29
30	31					

September

Sun	Mon	Tue	Wed	Thu	Fri	Sat
		1	2	3	4	5
6	7	8	9	10	11	12
13	14	15	16	17	18	19
20	21	22	23	24	25	26
27	28	29	30			

October

Sun	Mon	Tue	Wed	Thu	Fri	Sat
				1	2	3
4	5	6	7	8	9	10
11	12	13	14	15	16	17
18	19	20	21	22	23	24
25	26	27	28	29	30	31

November

Sun	Mon	Tue	Wed	Thu	Fri	Sat
1	2	3	4	5	6	7
8	9	10	11	12	13	14
15	16	17	18	19	20	21
22	23	24	25	26	27	28
29	30					

December

Sun	Mon	Tue	Wed	Thu	Fri	Sat
		1	2	3	4	5
6	7	8	9	10	11	12
13	14	15	16	17	18	19
20	21	22	23	24	25	26
27	28	29	30	31		

Time Goes By

A calendar shows days that have passed and days that are still to come. The day after today is called **tomorrow**. Imagine today is Wednesday. What day of the week would it be tomorrow? The day before today is called **yesterday**. What day of the week was it yesterday? It was Tuesday.

Tuesday
yesterday

Wednesday
today

Thursday
tomorrow

JULY

SUNDAY	MONDAY	TUESDAY	WEDNESDAY	THURSDAY	FRIDAY	SATURDAY
29	30	1	2	3	(4)	5
6	7	8	9	10	11	12
13	14	15	16	17	18	19
20	21	22	23	24	25	26
27	28	29	30	31	1	2

Imagine today is Friday. What day will it be tomorrow?

19

Years

There are 365 days in one year. A year also has 12 months. On a calendar, a year begins on January 1st. You can start counting a year from any date on a calendar. The time between your last birthday and your next birthday will always be one year.

Activity Box

Every four years, there is a **leap year**. In a leap year, February has one extra day. If 2012 is a leap year, when will the next leap year be?

This calendar shows June 2008.

SUNDAY	MONDAY	TUESDAY	WEDNESDAY	THURSDAY	FRIDAY	SATURDAY
1	2	3	4	5	6	7
8	9	10	11	12	13	14
(15)	16	17	18	19	20	21
22	23	24	25	26	27	28
30	1	2	3	4	5	

The time between June 15th 2008 and June 15th 2009 is one year.

SUNDAY	MONDAY	TUESDAY	WEDNESDAY	THURSDAY	FRIDAY	SATURDAY
31	1	2	3	4	5	6
7	8	9	10	11	12	13
14	(15)	16	17	18	19	20
21	22	23	24	25	26	27
28	29	30	1	2	3	4

Twelve months are equal to 365 days. A leap year has 366 days!

2008

Glossary

afternoon The time that follows the morning

calendar A chart that shows days, weeks, and months

clock A tool used to measure time

face The part of the clock that has the numbers 1 through 12

hand The part of a clock that points to numbers for hours and minutes

hour 60 minutes

hour hand The short hand on a clock that points to hours

leap year A year with one extra day, which happens every four years

minute 60 seconds

minute hand The long hand on a clock that points to minutes

month Usually 30 or 31 days

morning The time between sunrise and noon

night The time after the sun goes down

second hand A long, thin hand that counts seconds

skip count To count by numbers other than 1

tomorrow The day after today

watch A tool that people wear that tells the time

year 12 months

yesterday The day before today

Index

Printed in the U.S.A. — CG